Cryptocurrency

The Comprehensive Guide On How To Implement The
Very Best Strategies And Tricks To Make The Most Of
Your Nft And Cryptocurrency Profits

*(Learn How TheBlockchain Could Benefit Your Life, Your
Company, And Your Cryptocurrency Wallet)*

Thorsten Ludwig

TABLE OF CONTENT

What Exactly Is Meant By The Phrase "Double Spend Problem"?

The issue of double spending may be understood most well by considering the case of a photograph stored on a mobile device. If I post it on Facebook, then I have effectively created a replica of it. This did not really affect my budget at all. After that, I'll be able to post it on Instagram as well. Once again, at very little if any expense. I recently "double-spent" my photo, but no one seems to care since it does not truly influence anybody in a negative manner and hence is of little concern to them. Because of this, nobody cares how many times I post the same thing—whether it's once, twice, or even a hundred times.

Imagine for a moment that there is a kind of virtual money known as the Julian-Coin. Bob gives his buddy A one hundred of his Julian-Coins despite the fact that he only has one hundred. In the same way as with the photo, Bob just clicks "copy" and "paste," and he now gets one hundred more Julian Coins at absolutely no further expense. Now, he hands out the additional one hundred Julian Coins to a different acquaintance. He did very much the same things with the money as he did with the picture; the only difference is that this time, his pals care since money is a form of worth and trust. If we want to have a decentralized (meaning there is NO central institution) monetary solution, we need to discover a means to prevent double-spending without having a governing body. In a conventional financial system, a bank would make sure that Bob could not have done that, but if we want to have a decentralized solution, we need to find another approach.

In 2008, a person or group known as Satoshi Nakamoto proposed a solution to the issue of double spending in the whitepaper titled "Bitcoin: A Peer-to-Peer Electronic Cash System" (https://bitcoin.org/bitcoin.pdf), which was published on the Bitcoin website. No one truly knows who or what Satoshi Nakamoto is. The revolutionary concept presented in the eight-page document is the use of a blockchain as a means to do away with the need for a central authority figure while simultaneously ensuring that no one can cheat.

Concentration, Time, and Dedicated Effort

Both day trading and swing trading demand a significant amount of labor and knowledge in order to generate consistent profits, despite the fact that the necessary information is not actually "book smarts." Finding a strategy that gives you an advantage or a benefit across a significant number of transactions and then consistently using that strategy is the key to profitable trading. Once you've identified such a method, you should then put it into action.

Along with many components and extensive training, certain publicly accessible information is already being sold, and an advantageous process may now initiate the production of pay. Because the prices of goods fluctuate on a daily basis in a manner that is distinct from their movement on the previous day, the broker need to have the ability to put their process into action under a variety of circumstances and to adapt it as the circumstances evolve.

This is a challenging test, and the only way to get predictable results is to practice an approach under a large number of different market conditions. This demands a significant investment of time and attention, and should ideally be practiced using a demo account first, before any real money is risked.

Whether you should engage in day trading or swing trading is also dependent on your personality. Day trading is often associated with higher levels of pressure, calls for sustained focus over extended durations, and calls for incredible levels of self-discipline. Day trading is most well-suited to those who like being on their feet for long periods of time, who have fast reactions, and who have hobbies such as playing video games and poker.

A slower pace is maintained throughout the swing trading process, with lengthier pauses between operations such as entering or exiting trades. Even today, it may be quite high pressure, and in addition to that, it takes an incredible amount of order and tolerance.

Swing trading is a more viable option for those who struggle to maintain focus since it does not demand as much concentration as day trading requires. Swing trading does not need quick reflexes since deals may be made after the market closes and prices have stopped moving. This eliminates the need for quick reactions.

Trading in both swings and days affords a broker the opportunity to be their own boss and enjoy the independence that comes with that. Brokers often gamble with their own accounts, and they are responsible for covering any losses or gains that are generated as well as subsidizing their own accounts. Because swing trading takes up less time than day trading does, some people believe that swing traders have more opportunities available to them in terms of their time.

Why Even Take Into Account The Option To Hold In The First Place?

Because the Active HODL strategy is focused entirely on the long game, it is imperative that you be mentally ready for it. Although it is possible in theory for any and all cryptocurrencies to fail or disappear altogether, the likelihood of this occurring right now is extremely remote. Their prices may plummet catastrophically, which is something that has regularly occurred in the past and will continue to occur in the future, particularly when large waves of legislation on the national level of significant countries (the United States of America, China, EU states, South Korea, and Japan) hit the cryptocurrency market. Prices will fall dramatically anytime this event takes place, thus the only issue that remains is when it will take place. As the old proverb goes, "death and taxes are the only things that are certain in life," and at the moment, governments are trying to figure out how the second part of this proverb can apply to the cryptocurrency markets.

However, the government has no intention of eradicating cryptocurrencies, and the reason for this is that it is physically impossible for them to do so. Bitcoin will continue to function in unknown areas within offshore territories even if its use is rendered totally illegal everywhere on the planet. Even though one bitcoin might only be worth $0.01 at that time, the cryptocurrency will continue to exist for as long as there is even a single mining operation that supports it. Bitcoin, along with the majority of the leading cryptocurrencies, appears to be simply too large to fail at this time and for the foreseeable future. In contrast to the widespread misconception that cryptocurrency tokens are created out of thin air, their value is actually derived from the amount of energy that miners consume.

That is the grounding in the actual world for the crypto assets. A cryptocurrency network will continue to exist so long as there are miners actively participating in it. At the moment, the Bitcoin network uses almost the same amount of power as the nation of Colombia. Since crypto assets are rooted in the real world, it is impossible for them to vanish overnight. They may lose value over time and become practically worthless, but as long as there is at least one mining rig that is running their code, they will continue to function normally.

To invest in cryptocurrency with the long game in mind requires a mindset that is capable of imagining passing down a single digital token to one's grandkids. In many ways, this mindset is required. The same imagination can envision the same token delivering their descendants a fortune fifty or one hundred years from now, even if it is simply as a digital antique piece (yes, in the future we will have digital antiques). If you think this to be very unusual or extremely improbable, then you should not invest in cryptocurrency; it is as simple as that. Also, if you are short on cash, this is not the method to make a lot of money. I keep emphasizing this point mainly because I am aware of how easy individuals can convince themselves that investing in cryptocurrencies is the solution to their financial woes. In nine out of ten instances, the situation will be exactly the opposite.

I cannot stress this point enough: investing in cryptocurrencies ought to be considered a luxury that is reserved for those who are in a position to afford it. In the short term, it poses an extremely high risk, and in the long term, its outcomes are highly unknown. If you take the "hold on to forever" strategy, you are essentially betting that the cryptocurrency phenomenon will not go away. You are taking steps to protect yourself from the emotion known as FOMO, which stands for the fear of missing out. This compulsion is a lot more risky than completely avoiding cryptocurrencyall together. If fear of missing out (FOMO) is blowing in your direction, you can find yourself taking on additional debt in order to "catch" the latest crypto-train to riches. The same worry caused a large number of people to find themselves in precarious financial situations, but at the same time it enabled a very small number of people to realize significant financial gains. On the other hand, the other set of people undoubtedly arrived at the same precarious situation sooner or later. As I've mentioned before, nobody stays lucky for good forever. If the worry that you will lose out on something is what motivates you to take action, you will inevitably make poor decisions, which will put an end to the fun you have investing.

The opposite of FOMO is the strategy known as HODL. Because it drives a stake through the heart of the FOMO vampire, it possesses a great deal of value. When you make an investment to HODL, you put yourself squarely in the competition. However, you may play it in a way that will not leave you penniless and will not require you to spend hours upon hours a day praying while staring at a computer screen while watching trade candlesticks go up and down. When you have it, you are involved in the game to the extent that you could perhaps profit from it, but you are not so deeply involved that you risk drowning in the game's murky and unexpected currents. You are not going to lose the game in a single night. Instead, under the most pessimistic scenario, it will slowly disappear over the course of several years.

Inasmuch as HODL does not guarantee anything, it is only natural that it comes with its fair share of problems and shortcomings. The cryptographic currency ecosystem is in a constant state of flux and transformation, even as the price movements within the markets are frequently unpredictable to an extreme degree. Nobody has a complete understanding of cryptography that would allow them to forecast the future. Nobody is always right since we are all still trying to figure it out as it develops. I'm afraid I have to do the same thing and tell you that the only thing I can guarantee with this eBook is to provide you with some information that is accurate to the best of my knowledge and a few thoughts that you should take with a grain of salt. Other than that, I can't promise you anything. However, the knowledge gained over the course of the past decade regarding the fluctuations of the cryptocurrency market, in conjunction with the reasoning of a global community that is interested in technology, demonstrates that HODL is the best of all the uncertain crypto investment techniques that are now available.

If you do decide to put it to use, I wish you the best of luck. I am not just saying this because of you, but because of everyone else that has this belief out there.

This Study Will Serve As The Foundation For Cardano.

Cardano tends to stand out among its rivals in the proof-of-stake consensus algorithm as well as other major cryptocurrencies because of this rigorous approach. Cardano is another cryptocurrency that has been dubbed the "Ethereum killer," as its blockchain is rumored to be capable of handling more transactions than Ethereum's.

Having said that, Cardano is still in its early stages of development. In spite of the fact that it has beaten Ethereum to the proof-of-stake consensus architecture, it still has a ways to go before it can be used in decentralized financial applications.

Cardano aspires to become the world's financial operating system by delivering decentralized financial products that are comparable to Ethereum and providing answers for chain interoperability, voter fraud, and the illustration of legal contracts, amongst other problems. Cardano has the sixth-largest earner in market capitalization at $57 billion as of November 2021, and one ADA deal has been completed for about $1.79.

Polkadot (Dot) Polkadot is a one-of-a-kind cryptocurrency that uses the proof-of-stake consensus method and aims to deliver interoperability with different blockchains. Its protocol was designed to ensure the safety of permissioned and permissionlessblockchains and oracles, making it possible for multiple systems to collaborate and operate under a single roof. The primary function of Polkadot is its relay chain, which makes it possible for many networks to communicate with one another. Additionally, it allows for "parachains," which are parallel blockchains that have their own native coins and are designed for particular use cases.12

In contrast to Ethereum, developers working on Polkadot are not limited to the creation of decentralized applications; rather, they are free to build their own blockchains while taking advantage of the safety measures currently in place on Polkadot's chain. With Ethereum, developers are able to establish new blockchains; but, they are also required to create security measures, which leaves newer and more modest projects vulnerable to assault. The more nodes that are added to a blockchain, the greater its level of security. The concept of shared security can be understood when applied to Polkadot.

Gavin Wood, another one of the core founders of the Ethereum project, was the one who came up with the Polkadot protocol. However, Gavin and the other core founders had divergent perspectives on the future of the project. Polkadot's demand capitalization is approximately $41 billion as of November 2021, and the company has one DOT contract worth $39.13 billion.

Bitcoin Cash, often known as Bch,

The fact that Bitcoin Cash (BCH) is one of the earliest and most successful complex splits of the original Bitcoin gives it a prominent position in the annals of the history of alternative cryptocurrencies. A fork is an event that can take place in the realm of cryptocurrencies as a result of disputes and discussions held between miners and developers. Because digital currencies are not governed by a central authority, it is necessary for there to be widespread changes made to the code that underpins the token or coin at the time of writing. The method by which these changes are implemented differs depending on the digital currency in question.

When various groups are unable to come to an agreement, the digital currency is occasionally split up. The actual chain will always use the same code, but the new chain will start off as an updated version of the previous coin, complete with new code. The original chain will always use the same code.

As a result of one of these divisions, BCH started its existence in August of 2017. The debate over the issue of scalability was what prompted the development of Bitcoin Cash (BCH). The Bitcoin network has a limit of one megabyte (MB) for the size of each block in its blockchain. The size of each block will rise from one megabyte (MB) to eight megabytes (MB) as a result of the implementation of BCH. The rationale behind this change is based on the hypothesis that larger blocks will be able to accommodate a greater volume of transactions, which will in turn lead to a faster overall network.14 It also brings about other changes, one of which being the elimination of the Segregated Witness protocol, which has an impact on union space. As of the month of November 2021, Bitcoin Cash has a market value of approximately $10.5 billion and a price per token of $555.15.

Currency That Has Been Devalued.

Voltaire predicted that the intrinsic value of paper money, which was zero to begin with, would eventually return. All fiat currencies are issued either by their own governments or by various central banks. This money is a representation of abstract ideas such as faith and credit. On the other hand, a fiat currency by itself has no value that can be maintained over time.

When more and more currency is issued, fiat currencies have a natural propensity to lose some of their purchasing power over the course of some period of time. This phenomenon is exacerbated in monetary systems that are based on fractional reserve banking and schemes of fiat currency that are based on debt. In the schemes that are based on debt and use fiat currency, the currency will need to be either inflated or deflated;

otherwise, the system will fail and the debt-based schemes will fail.

All of those responsible for the currency would end up creating more than is required in order to maintain a constant price or to maintain stability in economic activities. This would result in an undesirable situation. The upshot of this would be price instability, as well as economic volatility. A reduction in the value of the currency would, in the long run, bring the entire economic structure of that particular society into disrepair.

The process of redistributing one's riches

An increase in the total amount of currency in circulation will only cause a distortion in the distribution of money, which in turn will cause a redistribution of purchasing power. This will, in effect,

21

take wealth from a significant portion of the population in order to serve the interests of a select group of individuals. When compared to the creation of additional money, redistribution of wealth will only result in a decrease in the overall amount of wealth in a society.

Despite the fact that it is being done for a noble cause, the government's deficit spending will lead to an increase in the total quantity of money as well as a devaluation of that currency. The way the government handles its deficit spending is dishonest, and it comes with a hidden tax that is levied on everyone who saves money and works for a living.

Wealth accumulated in fewer hands

Those who have the advantage of being able to manufacture currency will, over the course of a certain amount of time, be in a better position to amass wealth and property thanks to the schemes using fiat currency. As a consequence of this, there will be a greater concentration of wealth within society. It would be detrimental to the political and economic stability of an economy if there was an excessive concentration of wealth in that sector.

A single person with a million dollars in their savings wouldn't be able to purchase as many consumer goods, automobiles, or home appliances as 10 households that each have an income of one hundred thousand dollars.

Threat to morality

The presence of power almost always results in corrupt behavior, and full authority almost always results in complete depravity. It is monetary monopolies, such as loans, that give rise to the creation of fiat currencies; these currencies make it possible to acquire something at an almost insignificant cost. Because of this, the individuals who are accountable for the creation of fiat currency would be in a position to have a significant amount of influence over the political and economic environment.

It is impossible for human beings to be responsible stewards of a monetary system that would provide one segment of society access to all of the resources necessary to get something for nothing at all. In point of fact, all of those cultures that are ruled by the immoral schemes of fiat currency will eventually establish a pattern of getting something for nothing – a culture of entitlement; this is a society in which everyone is focused on living at the cost of the other rather than focusing on the development of wealth.

The evils of corruption

The fact that fiat currencies foster cronyism and corruption is one of the risks associated with using them. The end result of this would be the establishment of a culture that is tainted with corruption. Who will be in charge of maintaining a watchful eye on those individuals who are supposed to be the guardians? The annals of history are replete with examples of the numerous evils that can arise from having total power as well as instances of monetary abuses that can lead to the downfall of an entire economy.

In the previous 10 decades, the leading cause of death has been murder by another human being. The use of fiat currency is associated with an increase in the poverty rate experienced by the population. These mechanisms assist in the redistribution of wealth in such a way that they result in the formation of a wealthy minority that is not responsible for the generation of any wealth.

A breakdown in confidence

It is a difficult uphill struggle to retain the perception of having a specific value when there is an economic collapse regardless of the increasing prices. Given that the worth of fiat currencies is primarily subjective, this value perception can be difficult to maintain. The faith and trust that the general public has in those responsible for the system determines whether or not a country can successfully use a fiat currency.

When a fiat currency system has been abused, the faith of the population in that system will fail, and the money will simply revert back to the value that it had when it was first introduced into circulation. The item has no worth in and of itself. The upkeep of public confidence would be prioritized as the primary objective of any monetary policy that was founded on the fiat currency system. For example, behavioral economics has emerged as a powerful instrument that may be utilized in the formulation and execution of fiscal and monetary policy.

Because of this, the reporting on the economy that was provided by the government, the central banks, and the media would not be objective. The management of various perceptions has the effect of being able to influence the subjective condition of all people who would use the fiat money in order to maintain its perceived worth. This is because of the effect that the management of numerous perceptions has. Even when it is done well, perception management is one-sided, and when it is done poorly, it is nothing more than propaganda.

Taking Into Account The Central Authorities

Certain aspects of this transaction are remarkably similar to others that have occurred in the past. If you want to get into a bar, you need to be over the age of 21, and you have to pay the cover price (unless the bouncer at the entrance is a friend of yours). It is true that you can accomplish this right now using a credit card or any one of a number of other digital instruments; however, if you were to accomplish this right now, you would be leaving a vast data trail behind you. You would be giving your driver's license to an unknown person. You would be required to pay using a credit card, and the transaction would have to be authorized by a centralized authority. This authority would already be in possession of all of your personal information, in addition to a profile detailing everything you've ever purchased using that credit card. You would be using a smartphone that is connected to the network of a commercial carrier today, and that carrier not only has access to all of your personal information but also has compiled a massive profile of everywhere that phone has been, including a list of everyone you have ever called or texted as well as all of the data from every data collection opportunity that you neglected to opt out of.

In the absence of Central Authorities

Compare and contrast that experience with the experience that we have postulated, which is trustless and decentralized. In this scenario, the radio in your phone may still be connected to a carrier, but in order for your digital wallet to function, internet connectivity is not required. It might link to the club through unlicensed 5G airwaves, WiFi, or Bluetooth, among other connectivity options.

The Gain of Confidentiality

Consideration should also be given to additional aspects of data privacy and sovereignty. To begin, the club owner does not have access to any supplementary data. There are only two things that the owner of the club should be aware of. Are you over the age of 21? Have you forked over the required cover charge? In this instance, your private, immutable, and decentralized identification verified that you were older than the legal age requirement without disclosing your actual age or any other information about you. Second, it wouldn't make a difference whether one of your pals was working the front of house when you arrived since the funds (in the form of ADA) would be transferred immediately and irrevocably from your digital wallet to the club's digital wallet as a condition to open the door and let you in. This was a requirement for the club to be able to open the door and let you in. No deception allowed! There was a clear exchange of the monetary resources.

This is merely a starting point for your thinking; you may easily develop it much farther. There is a possibility that a Dutch auction will take place for a restricted number of NFT club tickets. These NFTs, which are smart contracts by definition, might have been created in such a way as to incorporate promotional materials for the artist that was playing that evening. It would have been possible to construct loyalty schemes. In actuality, if you can dream it up, you can put it into a smart contract in some form or another. It's possible that the NFT will include payment vouchers for the two-drink minimum, along with discounts and other types of incentives.

Individuals All Over the World Being Given More Agency

Imagine a world in which you are able to freely integrate your ideas, your abilities in social media and social video, your business skills, and all of the other creative energy that makes you wonderful and unique. This is the next phase of this concept. Then, the majority (or all) of the friction that has been placed on us by the central authorities that we have been compelled to deal with should be eliminated. This future will arrive in a matter of weeks at most.

The family of technologies that make decentralization possible holds the potential to deliver to us new degrees of financial freedom, personal data sovereignty, and a plethora of options.

The Complete List OfCryptocurrencies

Since Bitcoin was first made available, the use of cryptocurrencies has seen a meteoric rise. Even if the exact number of active cryptocurrencies is subject to change and the value of individual cryptocurrencies is subject to extreme swings, the market value of all active cryptocurrencies as a whole is generally moving in an upward direction. There are hundreds of cryptocurrencies that are actively traded at any given time.

The cryptocurrencies that are going to be discussed in this article are characterized by widespread adoption, significant user activity, and a relatively substantial market capitalization (in most cases, greater than $10 million):

1. BTC (Bitcoin)

Bitcoin is the cryptocurrency that is used the most all across the world, and it is often regarded as being the cryptocurrency that brought the movement into the mainstream. Its total market capitalization and the value of each individual unit consistently outweigh (by a factor of ten or more) those of the next most popular cryptocurrency. Bitcoin is designed to have a maximum supply of 21 million coins at any given time.

There is a growing consensus that bitcoin can function as a valid medium of exchange. Although many well-known businesses now accept Bitcoin as payment, the majority of them still work with an exchange in order to get their funds converted into U.S. dollars before they are released.

2. Litecoin (LTC)

Litecoin was first introduced in 2011, and it shares the same fundamental structure as Bitcoin. The key differences are a higher programmed supply limit of 84 million units and a shorter target block chain formation time of two and a half minutes. Both of these differences are outlined in the following table. The algorithm for encrypting data is also somewhat modified from before. In terms of market capitalization, Litecoin is typically regarded as the second- or third-most popular cryptocurrency.

3.Ripple Ripple is known for its "continuous ledger" system, which dramatically sped up the time needed for transaction confirmation and block chain creation. There is no formal target time for Ripple, but the average is every few seconds. Ripple was released in 2012. Ripple is also more easily converted than other cryptocurrencies, as it has an in-house currency exchange that can convert Ripple units into popular currencies such as the U.S. dollar, the yen, and the euro.

Critics, on the other hand, have pointed out that Ripple's network and code are more susceptible to manipulation by skilled hackers and might not provide the same level of anonymity safeguards as cryptocurrencies that are derived from Bitcoin.

4.Ethereum Initially released in 2015, Ethereum introduced a number of significant enhancements to the fundamental architecture of Bitcoin. In particular, it makes use of so-called "smart contracts," which mandate the completion of a specific transaction, require the parties involved not to back out of their agreement, and have a mechanism for refunds in the event that one of the parties breaches the agreement. Although "smart contracts" are an important step toward addressing the lack of chargebacks and refunds in cryptocurrency, it is not yet clear whether or not they will be sufficient to solve the issue entirely. This is despite the fact that these contracts are a significant step.

5. Dogecoin (DGC)

A variant of Litecoin, Dogecoin is easily identifiable by its mascot, a ShibaInu. It was created by the same people that created Litecoin. It has a shorter block chain creation time (one minute) and a vastly bigger number of coins in circulation - the creator's target of 100 billion unit mined by July 2015 was accomplished, and there is a supply limit of 5.2 billion unit mined every year thereafter, with no known supply limit. Additionally, there is no known supply limit. Dogecoin is notable for being an experiment in "inflationary cryptocurrency," and industry experts are keeping a careful eye on it to determine how the long-term value trajectory of Dogecoin compares to that of other cryptocurrencies.

6.CoinyeCoinye was created in 2013 under the original moniker "Coinye Wet," and is distinguished by an uncanny resemblance to the hip-hop superstar Kanye Wet. Wet's legal team became aware of the existence of the currency early in 2014, just prior to the debut of Coinye, and they promptly sent its creator a letter demanding that they stop making the currency.

In order to avoid legal action, the developers removed "West" from the title, changed the logo to a "half man, half fish hybrid" that resembled West (a sarcastic reference to a "South Park" episode that made fun of Wet's naive ego), and continued with the release of Coinye as they had originally intended. A cult following emerged for the currency among those who are enthusiastic about cryptocurrencies as a result of the hype and ironic humor that surrounded its release. In spite of this, West's legal team went ahead and filed a lawsuit, which forced Coinye's creator to liquidate their assets and close down the website.

Despite the fact that Coinye's peer-to-peer network is still operational and the platform is technically mine the currency, person-to-person transfers, and mining activity have all ground to a halt, bringing the value of Coinye to a position where it is essentially useless.

AN ENTICEMENT.

An inducement is a motivation or consideration that drives one to action or to more or more effective activities. Its meaning is a "motive or consideration that leads one to action." In the foreign exchange market, enticement refers to the practice of banks deceiving traders who are impatient to engage into the wrong move by allowing them to take or join trades that they do not want to or feel like taking; we will be seeing some examples of inducement in the very near future.

What exactly is the inducing of?

When we are getting close to a point when there is high demand or supply, the primary goal of banks and other financial organizations who participate in enticement is to cause customers to lose even more money. Keep in mind that the institutions want to make money off of the foolish money before they deliver the price in the direction that they want it to go.

If you have been following along with this e-book, you will know that this was the reason I was stressing the importance of being patient in earlier chapters.

Inducement is a technique that is used to trick buyers or sellers into believing that the market is about to move, and then the market moves against them before mitigating the desired demand or supply level, leading them to believe that the demand zone or order block zone will not be mitigated and forcing them out of the market. I see this as a form of liquidity grab, but it is more advanced because there are no support and resistance areas. Let's get moving!

CHART EXAMPLE NO. 18: INDUCEMENT.

Forex, or foreign exchange, is a market that moves money from people who are impatient to people who are patient, as we can see clearly now. Those who are impatient will believe the supply zone won't hold again, and so they will also join the selling, although the actual transaction is just a false sale to induce the sellers in the market. We have seen how inducement looks like; it almost touches the supply zone and then takes off as soon as possible.

Because we are astute money traders, we ought to know by now that if there is incentive in the market, there is a high likelihood or probability that the supply zone will contain almost 90% of the total. This is something that we should already be aware of. Why, because we now know that it was a fake sale to draw traders into doing sell trades before mitigation, but just by looking at this, we can see that the sellers will have gained some money before it went against them, and we can see how the supply zone actually played out. Why, because we now know that it was a fake sell to lure traders into taking sell trades before mitigation.

Let's look at some additional illustrations to help us get a better grasp on the topic.

CHART EXAMPLE 19: THE INFLUENCE OF.

Repeating the same thing over and over again until you become accustomed to it, enticement is now functioning as a confluence and informing us that the demand zone is stronger without the need for any other unique signs. Because we are accustomed to carrying out the rites, the chart is providing us with instructions on what to do, hahaha. In some cases, inducement can take the form of a wick coming dangerously close to touching the zone before retreating and then returning to properly ameliorate the situation. Because we won't be using all of the pairings for the back test, it's possible that we won't see an example like this one here. I simply mentioned it to let you know that the wick sometimes acts as an incentive and eliminates traders who are eager. Once the price reaches our primary point of interest, we want to eliminate the market as quickly as possible utilizing the entrance criteria that we wish to apply. It is important to keep in mind that the absence of inducement in the charts does not indicate that the demand or supply zone will not be maintained; rather, it only serves as confluence.

INDUCEMENT, an example of a chart 20.

Inducement is clearly more of a phony liquidity grab that takes place before the first movement; let's look at some examples including cryptocurrencies as well.

INDUCEMENT, an example of a chart, is seen here.

This event occurred on a cryptocurrency known as BNB USDT, and it serves as evidence that inducement can take place across all assets. Simply taking this into consideration, the incentive worked as a miniature support system, which resulted in the creation of liquidity. This is more like confluence telling you and indicating that there is more to happen on the zones below. Also, keep in mind that there are times when you have seen confluence but still hit SL. When this occurs, make sure that all of the trades you have entered are based on your trading plan. In this way, you will be able to look back and learn, as opposed to the situation in which you enter a trade at random.

When you accept a loss in accordance with your trading strategy, you should feel content and delighted. On the other hand, you should be aware that each trade you make outside of your trading plan brings you closer to financial ruin. At that time and with this knowledge, you know that you don't want to screw yourself up, so you just follow your trading plans. If you hit a loss outside of your trading strategy, then you should blame yourself for the loss.

SECURITY AROUND CRYPTOCURRENCIES

The security of cryptocurrency is composed on two distinct layers. The first component results from the challenging nature of locating hash intersections, which is a task that is performed by miners. The second possibility, which is also the more likely one, is an attack using the "51%" method. In this hypothetical situation, a miner who controls more than 51% of the network's mining power would be in a position to seize control of the global blockchain ledger and produce an alternate block chain. Even at this late stage, the attacker's options for what he can do are restricted. The attacker might either reverse his own transaction or stop other transactions from taking place.

A transaction hold may be placed on a cryptocurrency's account by an acquirer like as PayPal or by law enforcement. Cryptocurrencies are also susceptible to being seized by law enforcement. Every cryptocurrency features some level of pseudo-anonymity, and some coins even have additional features that allow for complete confidentiality.

Bitcoin's Legality and Taxation Cryptocurrency Legitimacy and Taxation

Despite the fact that cryptocurrencies are legal in most countries, Iceland and Vietnam are the only exceptions; Iceland is an exception mostly due to the fact that they have placed a freeze on its foreign exchange. However, cryptocurrencies are still subject to regulation and restrictions. Although cryptocurrencies are legal in Russia, it is against the law to buy anything with a currency other than the ruble. China has prohibited financial institutions from dealing with bitcoin, and Russia has legalized cryptocurrencies but made it illegal to buy anything with them.

The Internal Revenue Service (IRS) of the United States has ruled that Bitcoin should be treated as property for the purposes of taxes. This means that Bitcoin is now liable to taxes on capital gains. Guidelines for cryptocurrency have been issued by the Financial Crimes Enforcement Network (FinCEN). Those who "mine" bitcoins, also known as "miners," are cautioned in the updated guidelines about the possibility that they may be subject to legal action if they trade bitcoins for fiat currency. The updated guidelines include this crucial disclaimer. It says here:

"A person who creates units of convertible virtual currency and then sells those units to another person for real currency or its equivalent is engaged in transmission to another location and is a money transmitter." "A person who sells those units to another person for real currency or its equivalent."

It would appear that miners are included in this category, which might, in principle, render them subject to MTB classification. Bitcoin miners have expressed their confusion on this matter and have requested further explanation. To this day, this matter has not been discussed openly in a legal proceeding anywhere in the world.

Coins de cryptomonnaies Service (Service)

There is a plethora of information and monitoring services pertaining to cryptocurrencies that can be found online. The cryptocurrency market capitalization, price, available supply, and volume can all be viewed on CoinMarketcap, which is a good resource for doing so. Reddit is a fantastic platform for users who want to "follow trends" and "stay in touch with the community." There is a wealth of information available on CryptoCoinChart, including a list of cryptocurrencies, information on exchanges, details on arbitrage opportunities, and much more. Our very own website provides a list of crypto currencies along with the daily, weekly, and monthly percentage change in value that each has experienced.

Visitors to Litehack are able to view the network hash rate of a wide variety of cryptocurrencies using any one of nine distinct hashing algorithms. They even offered a graph of the network's hash rate, which allows you to identify any trends or indications that the general public's interest in a certain coin is either increasing or decreasing.

A mining guide website that may be found on CoinWarz. Given their hash rate, power consumption, and the going rate of the coin when it is sold for bitcoin, this ore can assist miners in determining which coin will yield the greatest return on investment if it is mined. You are even able to view the current and historical difficulty of each coin.

Acquire Your Own Knowledge. The more you know and the more you put that information to use, the better off you will be. This maxim applies equally well to the construction of a bookcase arrangement as it does to the management of electronic monetary contributions. Coin chase is so dedicated to expanding its knowledge of the world of virtual currencies that it has developed a social network for cryptocurrency management called Slicefeeds. This shows how seriously the company takes its mission. If you consistently engage in inefficient trading and are hesitant to use the resources available to you to your advantage, they will be there for you even though you will not use them.

Have some fun! You shouldn't just start your business and then spend all day sitting around looking at graphs. Engage in conversation with the close-knit financial experts you know and share your thoughts and experiences with them. Everyone will benefit from your increased financial success if you inject some zeal and humor into the process. It's not enough to just sit back and let life happen to you; instead, make the most of every moment by turning your endeavor into a rewarding and pleasurable experience, all while raking in millions of dollars.

Getting and Keeping Bitcoins If you want to start earning bitcoins, the first thing you need to do is get a bitcoin wallet, which is a digital wallet that can be used to transfer, receive, and store bitcoins. After that, you can buy and hold bitcoins. You can get one by using a service like "Coinbase" or "Blockchain" that is available online. Both of these bitcoin wallets are available in an online and a mobile edition, making them two of the most popular options. Having said that, establishing a wallet at your place of business would be the most secure approach to keep your cryptocurrency holdings for the foreseeable future.

Day Trading is quite similar to trading on the stock market; the only difference is that, rather than trading shares, you will be trading bitcoins. You should buy these Bitcoins when the price is cheap and then sell them after the price has risen significantly. The price at which you sell them ought to result in a sizeable profit for you. Naturally, because of this, it will be vital for you to keep up with the latest bitcoin news on a consistent and close basis. If you are prepared to put in the amount of work required to generate a profit from trading cryptocurrencies on a daily basis, then day trading might be the right choice for you. There is an abundant opportunity for financial gain. Making money in the stock market requires the ability to interpret charts and forecast price fluctuations.

Acquire Bitcoins with the receipt of interest payments - In the event that you already possess some Bitcoins, put those Bitcoins to work for you so that you can earn more Bitcoins. Earn Bitcoins through "investment" installments by lending out your Bitcoins to others. Directly lend money to a friend or acquaintance of yours. This gives you the ability to judge the truth of the situation, regardless of whether you consider the borrower to be reliable. After that, all that is left to do is for the two of you to reach an agreement on the conditions, such as the duration and the cost of the funding, and then you can get started. The disadvantage of this, however, is that you probably will not have an excessively large number of companions who meet your requirements for the loan amount, the term of the loan, and the loan cost. Regardless of this fact, it's a fun way to build up your Bitcoin balance.

Dissemination of There is also the option of using a Bitcoin loaning site, which typically includes postings from multiple borrowers. This website functions as a shared lending platform. Borrowers will send out solicitations for further finance, and you will be able to add to their credit. You can finance small amounts across a large number of credits to increase the default chance in this method. Credits denominated in traditional currencies, such as dollars or euros, function essentially the same way as those denominated in bitcoin. The borrower receives a predetermined amount of cash over a set period of time and is responsible for repaying the cash plus a premium. When you lend bitcoins to someone, there are a few things you need to know before you do so. First and foremost, the website where the loan is being made needs to be trustworthy. The information provided on the website about potential borrowers might become more reliable when the website has conducted a check on the candidates' financial health.

"Mining" is the process that generates new Bitcoins, and it may be used to your advantage to earn Bitcoins. When you mine Bitcoin, your personal computer searches for new blocks and adds new Bitcoin transactions to the blockchain, which is an open record that keeps track of all Bitcoin transactions. A document that contains the most recent recorded transactions is known as a block. Then, if your computer finds an additional piece of information, you will be rewarded with a certain quantity of Bitcoins. At this time, a block is comprised of 25 BTC. This value fluctuates at all times throughout history and goes down by a factor of 0.5 at predetermined intervals. Be aware that mining for Bitcoins is an expensive and time-consuming procedure, but that it has the potential to be financially rewarding in the long run despite these drawbacks.

Because trading is something that many of us are susceptible to being affected by fear, this is a very important lesson. When the price is climbing swiftly and the level of enthusiasm is really high, all we want is for there to be a downturn so that we can purchase some further shares with complete assurance.

"The presence of panic is a prerequisite for the bottoming process of any market."

Then, once the price has broken support and begun to fall lower, we begin to panic, and at that point, we are unsure whether or not we want to buy any more. Not only that, but now that we are considering selling, we are upset with ourselves since we did not take the profit while it was "at the top." The question that needs to be answered is how we can break the cycle of reactive trading.

When the market is in a free fall mode and it feels like everyone is giving up left and right, that is typically a fantastic moment to add some exposure to your portfolio. Because you should be following the basic rule of purchasing the blood and selling the greed when operating in this setting, the situation is beneficial.

"Training yourself to buy weakness, rather than selling into it, is one of the most difficult things to do," says an expert.

You have learned via your studies of technical analysis that it is a good strategy to purchase dips in up-trends, and you intend to put this knowledge to use. Knowing that you are buying weakness in an otherwise strong chart helps to keep you calm, and that is the voice that you hear in the back of your mind as you are doing so.

"The time to buy something is when no one else wants it, and the time to sell something is when everyone else wants it."

It is of the utmost importance to steer clear of the vicious cycle of purchasing high and selling low. If you find yourself constantly following tickers that are moving and then easily giving up after some consolidation, you are likely to watch your bankroll drain before your very eyes.

Your submission constitutes someone else's entry into the competition. The only thing that set them apart from you was that they exhibited patience, whereas you did not.

Before making a decision about what to do with each trade, you need to take into account the psychology of the market. When people are given up and emotion is low, the price usually represents a value. This is the case most of the time. If you get in early, you will probably be able to purchase a troubled asset for a price that is lower than its true worth. Always keep some extra cash on hand in case one of your favorite plays has a significant price decrease; so, when it does, you can buy the dip with full assurance.

"I sense some fear in the market; that means you should have cash ready in case we get any kind of flash dip," the analyst said. "I am sensing some fear in the market."

Invariability as well as Demonstrable Scarcity

Because NFTs are built on blockchain technology, the makers of NFTs can use smart contracts to limit the amount of NFTs that are issued while also imputing immutable attributes on their NFTs after they have been issued. For example, a developer can programmatically enforce the creation of a certain amount of a rare digital asset, just as such a developer can programmatically enforce the creation of an endless supply of a common digital asset. Another example would be that a developer can programmatically enforce the creation of a common digital asset.

In addition, by embedding certain digital assets on the chain, a developer can programmatically impose particular immutable attributes on those assets. This is particularly helpful for digital art assets that strongly rely on the verifiable scarcity of an original piece of artwork.

The ability to program

Programmability is one trait that non-fungible tokens (NFTs) and traditional digital assets have in common. This is one of the few similarities between the two types of digital assets. Before NFTs are made available to the public, it is simple to program in certain functionalities into them. For instance, CryptoKitties' tokenized virtual cats come equipped with a mechanism for reproducing themselves. This implies that a whole new cat can be bred by mating two existing cats together.

These days, creators of NFTs have a tendency to program complicated dynamics into their NFTs. Some examples of these features include random generation, forging, crafting, and redeeming. Within the realm of NFT, the options for programming are virtually limitless.

The Standards for Ethereum Tokens

Tokens on Ethereum can be used to represent anything, from lottery tickets to the talents of a character in a game to financial assets such as a company's share. Tokens can also be used to pay for things on Ethereum, such as transactions. Therefore, in order to create a thriving ecosystem on Ethereum or any other blockchain, it is necessary for each token to have the capacity to communicate and interact with the other tokens. For the sake of this example, let us assume that two different types of smart contract structures were used to create two different tokens. The developers of both tokens will need to thoroughly examine each contract before mapping out how each token will operate together, which will make scaling a bit more challenging than it otherwise would be. This is necessary so that the tokens can interact with each other. Imagine for a moment that there are a thousand unique tokens, each of which is accompanied by a thousand unique smart contracts. It will take an enormous amount of complicated calculations, which will take up a lot of time and will not result in an ideal scenario. This will be necessary in order to narrow down all of the requirements and requirements that are necessary to ensure that each of the one thousand tokens will be able to function together. For this reason, token standards were developed to define the rules that regulate the underlying architecture of a token on Ethereum'sblockchain. These regulations are governed by token standards. The acronym "ERC" refers to "Ethereum Request for Comment," which is the name given to these different sets of guidelines. While the number that comes after "ERC," such as

"ERC-20," denotes particular token standards, the acronym ERC stands for the Ethereum Token Standard.

The Challenges That Prompted The Development Of Blockchain Technology

Interference from a Third Party: Every transaction that needs to be completed with traditional fiat currency involves interference from a third party. For example, there needed to be a bank or a payment processor that would function as an intermediary between the many parties that required to conduct business.

Interference from the Government In the past, every nation's government was responsible for creating and regulating the money of their own country, which often times resulted in problems such as inflation. In the course of the process, the worth of the money held by many law-abiding persons was diminished through no fault of their own.

Identity Problems: As I mentioned earlier, one of the most significant flaws in the traditional banking system is that customers are required to divulge a great deal of information about themselves or their businesses. This includes information that customers may not always feel entirely at ease divulging, but are required to do so because it is "standard procedure."

Even if you decide to use a payment processor such as PayPal, for example, you will still be required to link it to a bank account and a credit card. This means that regardless of whether you want to be able to disguise your identity or not, you will never be able to do so when using the traditional banking system.

Transaction Costs: The issue of transaction costs presents still another significant obstacle. If you needed to do any kind of business through the banks, you were required to pay a service fee because those institutions are in the business of making a profit.

These are some of the issues that prompted the development of the technology known as blockchain, as well as the cryptocurrency known as bitcoin.

Mining for cryptocurrencies

People who are active in monitoring transactions on large blockchain networks (including Bitcoin, Ethereum, Litecoin, and many others) are also given the responsibility of updating transactions on the system (in a digital general ledger) in exchange for some form of payment. This task is offered in exchange for the privilege of monitoring transactions.

In order for a miner to proceed with the updating of a transaction, they will need to work through a series of mathematical equations, which is all a part of the process of authenticating transactions.

Bitcoin miners receive approximately 25 coins, Litecoin miners receive approximately 12.5 coins, and Ethereum miners receive approximately 3 ethers. The first miner who is successful in solving the equation is given the opportunity to be the one to update the transaction on the system, and in exchange for their services, they are rewarded with a predetermined number of cryptocurrency.

Given that a single bitcoin is now worth thousands of dollars at the time that this article is being written, you can get an idea of how much a fortunate miner stands to receive for the efforts that they put into mining.

This incentive is what makes it appealing for more individuals to participate in monitoring transactions on the network - the more, the merrier. The more people who participate, the more reliable the transaction on the network will be, and the faster people will be able to receive approval to do transactions on the network.

Because of this, the entire system operates faultlessly and without difficulty.

Based on what we have discovered up until this point, it is abundantly evident that cryptocurrencies like bitcoin provide enormous prospects for investing. However, if you are just starting out, it's possible that you won't truly grasp all of the hubbub about bitcoin and other cryptocurrencies. Because of this, the following chapter is going to go over things in great detail so that you can get a good grasp on what it is that they are.

The Most Prominent Cryptocurrency Trading Platforms

Following is a rundown of the top five cryptocurrency exchanges based on a number of criteria, including user reviews, levels of safety and security, fee structures, levels of accessibility, and overall user-friendliness of the platform.

The Coinbase

This is one of the most well-known and widely used exchanges for cryptocurrencies all around the world. It was established in 2012 and since then has garnered a positive reputation, solid backing from respected investors, and the support of millions of customers. The Coinbase platform is extremely user-friendly and convenient. It enables users to purchase, sell, store, and spend cryptocurrencies in a risk-free environment. Coinbase allows users to trade in Bitcoin, Litecoin, and Ether. Additionally, it offers a mobile wallet application that is compatible with both iOS and Android. A mobile wallet can be used to purchase bitcoin, or users can trade with one another on the Global Digital Asset Exchange (GDAX), a subsidiary of Coinbase that allows users to buy and sell cryptocurrencies. Coinbase is most well-known for having strong security measures, moderate fees, and an intuitive user interface. The insurance that Coinbase provides extends to protect any funds that are held on the platform. However, Coinbase only supports a limited number of countries, offers a restricted number of payment options, and directs more technical users to their GDAX platform.

The Kraken

2011 saw the birth of this San Francisco-based exchange, which had its beginnings in the same year. Kraken has entered into a partnership with Fidor to establish what will be the first bitcoin bank anywhere in the world. Integration with Bloomberg terminals is another feature of this product. Kraken gives its users the ability to trade Bitcoin for a wide range of fiat currencies from across the world, such as the U.S. dollar, the Canadian dollar, the British pound, the euro, and the Japanese yen. In addition to Bitcoin and Ethereum, Ethereum Classic, Ripple, Dogecoin, Monero, Litecoin, Stellar, Zcash, and ICONOMI, Kraken offers a wide variety of additional cryptocurrencies. Kraken is most well-known for its excellent reputation, minimal deposit and transaction fees, respectable exchange rates, extensive feature set, support for users located all over the world, and excellent user assistance. It has a restricted number of payment methods, and its UI is not very user-friendly, so it is not ideal for people who are just starting out.

The Poloniex

Poloniex was established in 2014 and has since evolved to become one of the most successful cryptocurrency exchanges in the world as measured by the volume of trades. It gives users the ability to trade Bitcoin for more than

100 different cryptocurrencies of varying sorts. The process of opening an account with Poloniex is quick and uncomplicated. The platform provides more advanced users with access to more sophisticated analysis tools in addition to its user-friendly design and extensive feature set. When compared to other cryptocurrency exchanges, Poloniex's trading fees are among the most competitive. The user support is excellent, with a chat interface where users may ask for assistance from other users in the community. The conversation box is kept useful by moderators who remove any comments that are deemed improper. Poloniex also provides BTC financing and has an open application programming interface (API). The fact that Poloniex does not support fiat currencies is one of the exchange's major drawbacks.

Shift your form

Shapeshift is an instant cryptocurrency exchange that was established in 2013. This exchange gives customers the ability to trade one type of cryptocurrency for another type of cryptocurrency. Shapeshift is compatible with Bitcoin in addition to a number of alternative cryptocurrencies such as Ethereum, Dash, Dogecoin, Monero, and Zcash. Regrettably, Shapeshift does not support any kind of trades involving fiat cash and cryptocurrencies. People are able to trade cryptocurrencies using Shapeshift while still retaining a high level of anonymity, which is one of the most significant benefits of using this service. Users are able to engage in the trading of cryptocurrencies without first having to form an account. Even worse, it does not keep any of its funds on a centralized exchange. It has a high reputation, a user interface that is suitable to newcomers, fair costs, and it supports dozens of different cryptocurrencies. Shapeshift also supports dozens of different cryptocurrencies.

The LocalBitcoins marketplace.

This is a well-liked peer-to-peer (P2P) market that brings together Bitcoin buyers and sellers located in the same city or region geographically, with support for thousands of locations across the world. Using LocalBitcoins, buyers and sellers can negotiate the terms of the transaction, including the manner of payment they prefer and whether or not they will meet in person to complete the transaction. While buyers and sellers are free to negotiate their own exchange rates through the site, the platform does deduct a one percent fee from each transaction. The site employs a reputation rating system and keeps a public history of each user's trades in order to ensure the user's safety while utilizing the platform. Additionally, it has an escrow service that will hold onto the monies until the seller verifies that the transaction has been finalized before releasing the funds. There is no need to verify your identity in order to sign up for a LocalBitcoins account. It allows users to buy Bitcoins without incurring any fees, is user-friendly even for those with little prior experience, is accessible from anywhere in the world, and supports a variety of regional currencies. It is not an excellent choice for purchasing a significant amount of Bitcoin due to its high exchange rates, which is one of its primary drawbacks.

The IOTA (or MIOTA)

The concept of a blockchain is subject to a thorough redesign thanks to IOTA. The IOTA system relies on a tangle design, as opposed to the standard blockchain, which consists of a linked chain of individual blocks that individually store distinct information in a sequential order. Any given block will point to the two blocks preceding to it in a tangle, which creates a data collecting system that is incredibly robust and safe. This makes it possible to have a transactional system that can grow indefinitely. Because there are no blockages, there are also no charges associated with doing transactions. The potential for transactions to take place outside of the context of the world wide web is the final significant benefit that IOTA brings to the table. IOTA's plan is to integrate the "Internet of Things" (IoT), which stands for the Internet of Things.

IOTA has the potential to be a key driving force in the development of Internet-enabled home appliances that are able to connect with one another. This would facilitate the processing of transactions on the tangle while also making the life of the end user simpler. Due to the fact that IOTA is still in the process of being completely developed, it may be too soon to go into its particulars at this time; yet, the technology demonstrates a lot of potential.

The URL for the IOTA website is iota.org.

One monero

Monero, much like Dash, is designed to provide greater anonymity than Bitcoin, however it is possible that Monero is more successful at accomplishing this goal than Dash is. BitMonero was initially developed as a fork of the cryptocurrencyBytecoin. It was debuted in April 2014 under the name BitMonero, which was derived by combining the words "bit" and "monero," which is the Esperanto word for coin. Bytecoin was a fork of Bitcoin that placed an emphasis on users' privacy and continues to operate as a relatively tiny cryptocurrency.

Monero is loaded with a plethora of different privacy-enhancing features. First, ring signatures are used to conceal the address of the person's wallet that is sending Monero. As a result, it is impossible to trace the wallet that is sending the Monero. The next step is for a brand-new technology known as RingCT, which stands for Ring Confidential Transactions, to conceal particular details relevant to the transaction. This includes the amount of money that was moved. Last but not least, the address that is supposed to be received has also been obscured. Because of these privacy features, Monero was able to rocket its way into the top 10 cryptocurrencies by market value, reaching number 10 with a market cap of $1.7 billion.

Stratis has only just started trading, but it already has a market valuation of half a billion dollars despite having just recently made its debut. That is quite an accomplishment for someone who is just starting out in the world of cryptocurrencies. Two factors have contributed to the rise in popularity of

Stratis. To begin, the Stratis development platform enables for the creation of decentralized apps within the platform itself. This means that programmers have access to a whole new toolkit with which they may experiment with blockchains and cryptocurrencies. Stratis enables private companies the opportunity to construct their own blockchains, which may then interface with these new apps as well as the main Stratisblockchain. This feature is perhaps the most impressive aspect of Stratis. Anyone who is interested in experimenting with blockchains can take advantage of this straightforward entrance point into the realm of blockchains.

How Does The Bitcoin System Operate?

Bitcoin adheres to the following three rules that are standard for traditional currencies, sometimes known as fiats:

It ought to be difficult to make (currency) as well as to locate (gold and other valuable metals).

It should only be available in limited quantities.

It is necessary for the general public to acknowledge that it possesses value.

When analyzed, Bitcoin demonstrates that it possesses all three of the following qualities:

Bitcoin relies on intricate computer algorithms, which need a significant amount of processing power and a proof-of-work to validate transactions. It is difficult to recreate or copy successfully.

The total number of bitcoins in circulation is capped at 21 million at this time. As of 2015, about just two thirds had been mined.

There are hundreds of different exchanges for Bitcoin, and it's become one of the payment alternatives accepted by a wide variety of businesses, both large and small.

Miners of Bitcoin are offered the possibility of getting Bitcoin in exchange for the time and energy they put into the process. In contrast to fiat currencies, the supply of bitcoins will never increase, hence the cryptocurrency was designed from the start to be a deflationary medium of exchange. Once the available currencies have been mined, this, along with the decentralization concept, ensures that no one, not even the government, can create any more money. The value of the currency will continue to rise even after all of the coins have been mined out of the ground.

We now know that transactions involving bitcoin are being recorded in a digital ledger that goes by the name of a blockchain. The idea of decentralization lies at the heart of what makes Bitcoin such a useful cryptocurrency. The result of blockchain's decentralization is that no one, not even the government or large corporations, can claim ownership of it. Transactions are broadcasted publicly across the whole network, which helps to ensure that both parties have met their obligations under the agreement. The code is freely available to the public, similar to the Android Operating System or Linux. It would be accessible to everyone, ensuring complete openness and candor.

The blockchain is protected against threats posed by many points of entrance, and it is resilient against threats posed by multiple points of failure, thanks to decentralization. Consider the following scenario: you are presented with one Bitcoin. You may examine the records quite easy to ensure that the Bitcoin transaction you are receiving is legitimate and to verify that the amount you are receiving has not yet been spent. The only costs associated with transactions will be the cost of the electricity or mining power required to keep the blockchain operational.

This has a number of important applications in the real world, including the facilitation of cheaper international payments and the reduction of the overall price of various goods and products.

Cryptocurrency Mining

You may be perplexed as to why some individuals would voluntarily provide their services to update transactions on a blockchain network and why they would want to trouble themselves with the solution of mathematical equations in order to add new blocks to a blockchain network. The mining of cryptocurrencies provides a straightforward explanation for this phenomenon.

The connected nodes on the blockchain network are known as miners, and they are the ones who are responsible for keeping the transactions on the blockchain network up to current. Miners participate in this activity because it provides them with rewards.

Because miners are rewarded with 25 new bitcoins for each new block that they upload onto the network, the blockchain network is designed to function as an incentive-based system. Bitcoin miners are those that contribute to the network by uploading transactions, earning rewards for their efforts, and assisting in the distribution of newly minted bitcoins.

Therefore, miners engage in a vigorous competition with one another to solve the equations correctly. The miner who solves the equations first is the one who gets to be the one to upload the new block into the blockchain network, which contains information about a new transaction, and also gets to be the one to win 25 new coins.

At the time that this article was written, the value of a single bitcoin was close to $14,000. That should be enough of an incentive for anyone interested in being one of the nodes that monitor and update transactions on the blockchain network to maintain their interest.

As you are aware, the technology of blockchain makes it possible to have a decentralized currency that can be used securely in private, free from interference from governments, and on an international scale.

The Original Brains BehindBitcoin And Other Cryptocurrencies

The name Satoshi Nakamoto was used by the person or people who are still unknown but are credited with the creation of Bitcoin and its first reference implementation. In addition, they developed the very first blockchain database as a component of the implementation. In the course of the procedure, they were the first people to solve the problem of double spending with the digital currency. Up until December of 2010, they were actively participating in the creation of Bitcoin.

Nakamoto asserted that he was a male resident of Japan who was born on April 5th, 1975. Speculation, on the other hand, has mostly centered on a number of non-Japanese cryptography and computer science experts who are currently residing in the United States and Europe. These individuals are seen to be the most likely candidates to be Nakamoto.

As of the 24th of May in 2017, it is believed that Nakamoto possessed up to about one million Bitcoins, with a value estimated at approximately $4.7 billion USD as of August 2017.

In October of 2008, Nakamoto published a paper at metzdowd entitled "The Cryptography Malay Language."com providing an explanation of the Bitcoin digital currency. Bitcoin: A Peer-to-Peer Electronic Cash System was the title of the document. Nakamoto released the first Bitcoin software in January 2009, which simultaneously launched the Bitcoin network and the first unit of the Bitcoincryptocurrency, which was simply named Bitcoin. On January 9, 2009, Satoshi Nakamoto published Version 0.1 of the Bitcoin software on SourceForge.

According to Nakamoto, work on the writing of the code initially began in the year 2007. The person who came up with the idea for Bitcoin was aware that due to the nature of the cryptocurrency, the core design would need to be able to accommodate a wide variety of transaction types. The implemented solution made it possible to use predictive scripting in order to enable parameterized code and data fields from the beginning of the process.

Nakamoto established a website with the domain name bitcoin.org and remained actively involved in the development of the Bitcoin software alongside a number of other programmers until the middle of 2010.

Around this time, he discontinued his involvement in the project, transferred several related domains to various prominent members of the Bitcoin community, and handed over control of the source code repository and network alert key to Gavin Andresen. He also stopped his involvement in the project. Nakamoto was responsible for all modifications to the source code up to a short time before his death and handover of the project.

HOW BITCOIN GUARANTEES YOUR ANONYMITY IN THE INTERNET WORLD

Bitcoin is decentralized and public ledgers are not kept private: "dentite" are not recorded anywhere in the Bitcoin protocol itself; nonetheless, every transaction that is performed using Bitcoin is viewable on the publicly distributed electronic ledger known as the blockchain.

The anonymity that Bitcoin affords users is simultaneously a selling point and a challenge for authorities charged with regulating financial markets. Its true level of anonymity will become an increasingly closely studied topic as the rate of adoption of the currency increases and as it comes under scrutiny by the legal and financial systems, particularly with regard to compliance with applicable anti-money laundering (AML) statutes and know-your-customer (KYC) controls.

Participation in the Bitcoin network requires a user's personal identification information to be linked to their Bitcoin holdings. The majority of Bitcoin users gain access to the cryptocurrency by using one of the numerous popular online wallets or exchange services. Although this loss of anonymity occurs at the point of entry into the currency and is not a feature of the Bitcoin protocol itself, it is important to note that for these users, Bitcoin offers no greater degree of privacy than a traditional bank account.

Those who want to take use of the inherent anonymity of Bitcoin will need to find an alternative entry point. This could involve purchasing Bitcoin in a private transaction, receiving Bitcoin as payment for goods or services rendered, or receiving Bitcoin as a reward for mining. Since real-world identities are not recorded on the blockchain ledger, further Bitcoin transactions can then be conducted in an anonymous manner: the only identifying information that is stored there is the Bitcoin address, and the owner keeps a copy of the accompanying private key to serve as evidence that they are the rightful owner.

Step one is to gain access to all of the other "web wallet" services by hacking into blockchain.info. Oh, but wait, aren't these businesses operated ethically, with a significant amount of money from venture capital? If you take into account the VC-funded RNG Improvement to the R code, do you believe that the company's other security measures are significantly improved? And while you're at it, go ahead and breach the Cognate...

Download all of the "aved web wallet" in the second step. Now, each of these wallets is encrypted using the user's private key, but it doesn't change the fact that the majority of them are protected by private keys that are only somewhat more complex than "123456." Therefore, you should begin throwing it at your password cracker. As a bonus, obtain the email addresses of all the other users and download the remaining password information. And let's get going...

Step 3: Now that we've gotten to this point, it's time to make yet another "improvement" to Blockchain.JavaScript notation for "nfo" Simply adjust things so that they will reveal passwords to you. Something subtle, something brutal, or something else entirely. Just so long as it does the job. The Bitcoin community, for whatever reason (perhaps a funny one), seems to believe that downloading JavaScript from a server in order to access your wallet is a more "secure" option than simply having all of your digital currency kept by someone else. However, this is not the case. Therefore, make it a point to giggle hysterically after each new paword roll.

Step 4 is to be patient. Young padawan, patience is a virtue you must cultivate. They will continue to work until your improvements are seen, nagging all the suckers who, for some reason, despite believing in a decentralized digital Clam, are not on trusting centralized companies because "the market will eliminate bad actor" or some other such Randian fantasy.

Step Five: After you have been found out, and only then, will you move all of the virtual Cubits into your own accounts. Conveniently, the wallet provider will notify you when you have been found out and let you know that you should transfer the loot since, well, they are going to have to post a big announcement and erase your improvements.

Step 6: Join the crowd on Bitcoin who mock those who lost their binary Ankh-

Moorpork Dollars to your attack. Everyone knows that you should only store your Bitcoins on your own personal computer, thus everyone else is laughing at those people. This computer must run a self-burned version of live Linux and must not be connected to the internet at any time. In point of truth, you absolutely must adhere the ethernet port cover. Don't forget to include posts pointing out how the thief is actually rendering a public service in the course of the object parade by enlightening the victims on how computer security functions.

Step 7: Now it's time to begin writing the malicious code module that will search for Bitcoin wallets. This pretty little malicious program should copy wallets that are encrypted as well as those that are not encrypted. It should additionally add an improvement to every Bitcoin client it finds to once again tell you the password. This should be done at least once more. Don't want to put in the effort to really write the infection procedures? Now, there are services that you may use; all you need to do is locate your friendly PPI service.

Step 8: If you crack a stolen wallet, do not attempt to steal the contents of that wallet. To put it simply, not right now. After all, an unsecured Bitcoin wallet is perhaps the best hot potato IDS, and you don't want the news to spread too quickly. Please hold on for a moment. Consider the impermanence of everything as you meditate. And once you get their cooperation, you should rob them cold.

Step 9: Become a part of the crowd on bitcoin that laughs at people who have lost their bankroll. A city known as Ankh-MoorporkBecause it is common knowledge that you should only store your Bitcoins in a paper wallet, you should include the Dollar symbol to your malcode. Once more, make certain to include a point in the subjectivist parade noting how the thief is performing a public service by educating the victim on how computer security works. This is an essential component of the objectivist parade.

Step 10: Make the most of your life!

Disputes Or Matters Of Controversy

When you peel back the top layer of NFTs, you'll find that there are other overlapping challenges, including environmental, logistical, ethical, and others.

Many people have brought attention to the effect (severe ecological impact) that the development of NFTs and trade explosions have on planets that are already in a degraded state as a result of climate change (climate change-related catastrophes, environment, racism, and inequality). What is the connection between non-financial transactions and the changing climate? Ethereum is a platform that supports a permanent blockchain that contains a large number of these NFTs. To put it another way, the process of generating NFTs, adding tokens to the blockchain, and the wave of transactions (bidding, resale, etc.) all take a significant amount of energy. When it is multiplied by a significant market that is motivated by greed, we are beginning new types of environmental damage. That was supposed to convert the system into a carbon-depleting form to the extent that it maintained its ability to operate safely, but this has not yet taken place. It is still uncertain when this switch will take effect.

The decision to sell a specific work of art as a non-financial transaction (NFT) may not be the best chance to capitalize on given its fairness and ethical implications. RJ Palmer, a digital artist, issued a warning about accounts that extract art by mining tweets from other artists and artists and selling them as NFTs. If the work of an aspiring artist is not adequately enforced or researched to see if the person authoring the NFT is the genuine artist, the originator, or the owner of the copyright, then the work of the aspiring artist might be horribly exploited. This has resulted in the creation of a setting in which the relative anonymity of bitcoin transactions may be abused, stolen, and otherwise damaged.

Take Informed Decisions Regarding Your Business.

In order to make the transition from traditional art to cryptographic art, meticulous preparation as a commercial decision as well as the selection of art dealers and galleries is required. Nifty Gateway is now the market leader in terms of sales volume, contributing to the crypto art industry's current valuation of $445 million. Due to the high level of competition, it is very necessary to get familiar with the language, choose the appropriate platform, and seek the advice of knowledgeable specialists. Do not yet concentrate on achieving a consistent or quick profit. It is strongly recommended that the profits from the sale of cryptographic arts not be used toward the payment of rent. As a result, there won't be any significant differences between it and the "old" art market.

According to studies, the amount of space required by a single computer to generate a single board of NFTs is equivalent to the amount of power that citizens of the EU use in a single month as a whole. This is a significant environmental effect. To put this in perspective, in the year 2020, the Louvre Museum utilized the same amount of power as 677,224 individual homes in Paris. It would be beneficial to use part of the money made from the art of cryptography toward supporting Jason Bailey's Green NFT awards and other initiatives that aim to reduce the amount of energy that is used by NFTs.

Experiment with one piece at a time, just as you would when working with a new media. It is a good idea to finish, embed, or produce activated encrypted art by playing it back in media, such as playing it as an animation in the format of.mp4 or.gif, adding music, or transforming a photo into interactive digital art. In this way, the artwork may be completed, embedded, or created. You may also build a series that is exclusive to NFTonly publications to determine which works are the most in-demand. We do tests and research to determine what would be most beneficial for your target collector as well as for you, all while adhering to your core beliefs and the community around your brand.

Therefore, as long as the legal repercussions are recognized, the non-traditional art market (NFT) may give an appealing alternative to the conventional art market. The selection of the market and the specific artwork that will be sold is the product of thorough study of the commercial, practical, and legal elements.

What Are The Advantages Of Dealing In Cryptocurrencies?

Trading cryptocurrencies comes with a wide range of advantages, some of which are listed below:

1. Unpredictability

The fact that cryptocurrency markets are so highly unstable, which is something that some people could consider a drawback, is also what makes trading cryptocurrencies so fascinating and enjoyable. Although there is a good risk that you may suffer a loss, there is also a good chance that you will make a significant profit.

2. Business hours and days

The cryptocurrency markets are open around the clock, and there is no certain period that traders must adhere to in order to participate. Because there is no one authority controlling the cryptocurrency market, traders are free to do business whenever and wherever they want. The only time a market is likely to be inaccessible is when it is receiving infrastructure changes or when it is being split off into a new market.

3. Increased financial flexibility

Because of the increased liquidity of the market, it is now possible to easily convert your cryptocurrency holdings into fiat money without having any effect on the value of the currency on the market. Increased liquidity results in improved pricing, which in turn leads to speedier transactions and higher precision in analysis.

4. Freedom of mobility

Trading in cryptocurrencies gives you the ability to go long or short without any restrictions. Your motion is totally unrestricted, and the decisions that you make are wholly under your control at all times.

CURRENT TRENDS

The year 2017 saw an unprecedented increase in the value of cryptocurrency. For example, the price of bitcoin skyrocketed from $429 USD in 2016 to $17,500 USD at its all-time high in 2017. This increase took place in a period of less than a year and made some fortunate investors become multi-millionaires. The surge in the value of cryptocurrencies may have been caused by a number of different things, but the most important one is probably the proliferation of online commerce and financial dealings. Because more and more people are moving their lives online, it stands to reason that the number of online currencies available to facilitate various online activities will also continue to grow.

The current flood of investors and the excitement that is being generated about it in the media may also be contributing factors to the price increase. The market as a whole was hit with a severe shock, which caused the price of each coin to rocket through the roof. The price of cryptocurrencies is only going to continue to go up as more and more people start investing in them.

However, despite the fact that everything seems to be going swimmingly, we've seen a very dramatic decline in 2018. This is because a number of platforms exited the market as a result of unsafe servers and "shady" transaction procedures, which is why we are in this situation. In essence, these businesses and platforms did not take the appropriate precautions to ensure the safety of their servers, which resulted in a significant burden being placed on their investors. As a consequence of this, the market reacted in a pessimistic manner. Before making a significant choice about your finances, it is crucial to take a step back and carefully consider the implications of your actions.

Checking the laws of the place you reside to see what they have to say about cryptocurrencies is one thing you can do to be sure everything is above board. Even if the cryptocurrency market is unregulated and outside of the control of the government, you still face the risk of encountering difficulties when trying to withdraw your coin holdings and convert them into fiat cash. Imagine what the authorities must be thinking when they see your bank account suddenly shoot up by $50,000 in a single day without any taxes being withheld; this may show up as a "under the table" transaction in certain jurisdictions, and you may be prosecuted with or subject to an audit for tax evasion or other financially illegal activities.

Step 2: Determine the necessary pieces of hardware. This has more to do with mining, but it doesn't hurt to find out what type of technology you'll need in order to invest in what you want. If you want to invest in anything, work out what kind of technology you'll need. There are certain types of investment programs that are only supported by specific search engines, and your present search engine may or may not be compatible with those search engines (for example, you require Windows but only possess a Mac). In other circumstances, there are investing programs that are supported by all search engines.

Step 3: Make a plan for your money. Figuring out how much money you will be adding to the account is the most important part of this process, even if it entails a number of other considerations as well. The main amount, or the amount of money you will begin with, is the most important factor to take into consideration. After that, choose a timetable to adhere to in terms of adding further funds to the investment, assuming that additional funds would be added at all. Determine how much you will be contributing to the investment at the end of each period (for example, every two weeks, every month, every six months, every year, etc.). Always make sure that you have enough money to support yourself in the event that things do not go the way you would want them to go.

**Once you've identified a time during which contributions may be made, be careful to adhere to it. Do not begin investing on a biweekly basis and then gradually increase it to a monthly one. Make sure that you are able to pay for your period without putting yourself in a difficult financial position.

Set up your account and wallet in the fourth step. It is time to start investing now that you have finished all of the planning that was necessary. Establishing any and all administrative accounts that are required in order to invest should be the first item on your to-do list. Once again, this is something that is entirely dependant on the currency that you are considering investing in as well as the platform that you are investing on. Concerning the wallet, you will need a location in which to keep your cryptocurrency. Even while there are wallets that can be accessed online, it is recommended that you invest in a hardware wallet instead. These may be difficult to find and can cost a significant amount of money, but they give you full control over your currency and significantly limit the chance of fraud or theft.

The fifth step is to begin investing. Therefore, now that you are equipped with the information and resources necessary to create money, it is time for you to really get out there and make some. This stage is not only the one with the most specific instructions, but it is also the most difficult to carry out. When you initially begin investing, you will face the temptation to invest all of your money at once and to sell at the first hint of a favorable return on your investment. Caution is advised, though, since the process of investing may be arduous at times. There is no assurance that you will earn a profit, and you may find yourself "bankrupt" in the blink of an eye if anything goes wrong. However, it is essential to keep in mind that things going well is also a possibility, therefore it is best to have a cheerful attitude.

Step 6: Stay up to date on the latest activities and trends in the industry. This is crucial because it enables you to choose when and where you should invest as well as the amount you should put in those investments. Do not be afraid to make some movements and invest elsewhere if you believe that a coin in which you have invested is going to perform badly or if you become aware of a change in another market that catches your interest. But you really must keep in mind that you need to be patient; you can't expect things to change overnight.

The seventh step is to reinvest any profits you receive from your investments. After you have earned some money, you shouldn't rush to deposit it and then go on an extravagant trip right away. Instead, you should put it back into the market so you may attempt to earn even more money. In the end, the more money you have invested in the market, the more money you will be able to earn from that investment. One profitable investment does not always translate to a profitable investing portfolio.

Step 8: Withdraw your funds immediately if circumstances continue to deteriorate. Taking your money and putting it somewhere else is the absolute last thing you should do in the event that things take a turn for the worst. Even though it is often difficult to identify impending unfavorable changes in the market, these adjustments may sometimes be anticipated. If you can anticipate its arrival, the prudent thing to do is remove all of your money from the situation. However, this is a hazardous option, and you need to be very certain that the market is likely to head in the wrong direction, which requires a great deal of research on your part.

Depending on how you play your cards, investing in the cryptocurrency market might either be lucrative or disastrous. In point of fact, everything boils down to one's level of luck and knowledge. Regardless of what you want the market to do, it will continue to go in the same direction it has been moving in. On the other hand, if you have the appropriate education, you have the ability to recognize these developments. And this is when you will wind up earning the majority of your money.

(such as gold or other precious metals).

2. They will only accept a certain quantity.

3. Other people need to recognize their worth in order for it to be valued.

Using Bitcoin (BTC) as an example, it satisfies all three of the following criteria:

1. The production of bitcoin involves the use of complicated computational procedures that need a significant amount of computing power. Because of this, it cannot be easily replicated or done at a minimal cost.

2. There are only 21 million bitcoins available for purchase at any one time.

3. As of the year 2015, around two thirds of this number have been mined.

4. The cryptocurrencyBitcoin is accepted almost everywhere, from Subway to OKCupid, and there are hundreds of exchangers for Bitcoin.

In most instances, traditional currencies, which are also known as fiat currencies, are differentiated from other types of money by the fact that they are not attached to a certain nation, country, or organization. There are no Bitcoins produced in the United States, there are no Litecoins produced in Japan, and there is nothing comparable. They are put into circulation.

Bitcoin was designed to be a "deflationary money," which means that its value should, in theory, increase over time as more people start using it. Unlike fiat currencies, which are susceptible to inflation and whose value will decrease over time due to the passage of time, virtual currencies do not lose value over time. After all, the value of one dollar in 1917 is comparable to twenty dollars and seventeen cents today. As a direct consequence of this, the value of one US dollar is equal to twenty times what it was one hundred years ago. To put it another way, if you save one dollar for the next hundred years, you will be able to purchase less and fewer goods with that dollar, but the value of bitcoin will increase over time rather than decrease. Another example from the real world is when Laszlo Hanyecz performed the first real-world transaction with bitcoin on May 22, 2010, when he paid 10,000 BTC for two pizzas in Jacksonville, Florida. This was the first time anybody had ever paid for anything with bitcoin. At the current exchange rate, 10,000 BTC is worth more than $40 million.

Bitcoin was developed in this manner so that no one individual or government could increase the amount of money, hence lowering the value of the capital that already existed. It is also important to keep in mind that the currencies based on fiat that we are most acquainted with today were not always the most important participants in the money market. For a very long time, gold and other precious metals were considered to be the most desirable forms of currency for day-to-day usage. The ability of governments to standardize and verify the metallic composition of coins was a prerequisite for the widespread adoption of coins and subsequent paper bills as a form of payment.

This is what the great economist John Maynard Keynes had to say about inflation and currencies that contributed to inflation.

"Through a process of persistent inflation, governments are able to stealthily and unobservedly appropriate a substantial percentage of the wealth of the people who are under their control. They confiscate without discrimination and at their own discretion, and although this process leaves many people impoverished, it leaves a select few with more wealth. Not only does the sight of this random restructuring of riches undermine one's feeling of security, but it also affects one's trust in the justice of the existing distribution of wealth in the world.

Looking at Bitcoin from the other perspective demonstrates the enormous potential it has, despite the fact that the decentralized nature of the cryptocurrency lends it an air of mystery. Because there is not a single authority that is in control of the money supply, all parties involved (including the government, businesses, and consumers) are compelled to be open and honest about the processes they employ, which reduces the likelihood of fraud or other forms of manipulation. Miners get compensation (in the form of currency) for their labor, which guarantees the network's transparency. Because of this one decisive factor, a large number of investors have a positive outlook on the long-term sustainability of the currency. One common line of reasoning put out by Bitcoin naysayers is that the currency may, in principle, be devalued due to the absence of any official support for it. However, this has occurred in the past with fiat money in hyperinflationary conditions, when governments can no longer guarantee the value of their currency and are forced to create a new one. We have seen this phenomenon before.

Because of the declining value of the money in the German Weimar Republic in the year 1920, banknotes were hung on the walls as wallpaper. Because of the present economic situation in Venezuela, which is experiencing yearly inflation of over one thousand percent, many of the country's citizens are unable to buy basic necessities like bread. Supporters of Bitcoin hold the belief that the money is immune to economic downturns.

The fees associated with foreign transactions are yet another domain in which cryptocurrencies excel above their conventional counterparts. Anyone who has ever been required to transfer money overseas is aware of how prohibitively costly it can be to carry out financial operations of this kind. These expenses might sometimes reach an astounding 10% of the total. Because there are no "nations" involved, cryptocurrencies do not handle international transactions any differently than they do local transactions. As a result, there are low costs associated with transferring money anywhere in the globe with cryptocurrencies.

It takes around ten minutes for a Bitcoin transaction to register, but it might take several days for an international bank transfer, and other cryptocurrencies are even quicker than Bitcoin.

Bitcoin was created in 2009, at the depths of the global financial crisis. Bitcoin was designed to function as a decentralized electronic money system, but it has also attracted investors interested in cryptocurrencies as a store of large value currency, comparable to gold in many respects. If Bitcoin were a country, it would be in the top 30 richest and most lavish countries in the world.

There will never be more than 21 million bitcoins in circulation since that is the maximum supply limit. When a digital currency is first given, its creator (or creators) have the ability to specify its parameters, which cannot be altered at a later time. These parameters might include how much of the currency is available, the rules for trading it, and how fresh Bitcoins are introduced to the market. Because of these rules, which have been in place since Bitcoin's inception, the total amount of bitcoins that will ever be available is capped, meaning that the cryptocurrency will always be a scarce commodity.

Since it has already been distributed, nobody, not even an administration or

Satoshi themself, can make any changes to that. Bitcoins are unique digital assets that cannot be duplicated or reproduced in any way. Because new minerals and pockets are discovered all the time, gold is constantly being added to the market, which means that it is only a somewhat scarce asset. This is the point when the connection with gold falls slightly level.

Bitcoin is a decentralized digital currency that uses cryptography to secure its transactions and to prevent its value from being altered by the actions of its users. Moving gold will need a significant financial investment (for things like a reinforced vehicle, enhanced security, and the expense of additional space at a secure workplace, among other things). A "cold wallet," also known as a "hard wallet," is essentially just a USB stick that a person uses to store their Bitcoins.

Investing as Opposed to Cash

According to the Bitcoin white paper, the cryptocurrency was designed from the beginning to function as an online currency. However, the unpredictability of the payment effectively and quickly rendered its one-of-a-kind goal irrelevant. To provide just one example, a "sane" person would never feel the urge to buy coffee with bitcoin. This is due to the fact that you may use Bitcoin today to buy an espresso that costs $3, but tomorrow the same amount of Bitcoin might be worth $30, meaning that you would have spent $30 on the espresso even if it was only worth $3.

Or, to look at it from the vendor's point of view: you use Bitcoin to pay for your $3 cappuccino, and the value of that Bitcoin drops to sixty cents the next day. After that, at that time, the seller lost out on the opportunity. Due to the extreme volatility of its value, it is almost useless as a system for managing electronic currency. As is the case with gold, people acquire Bitcoin not with the expectation that they will be able to go to a shop and spend it, but rather because they anticipate that it will maintain its value. In the same way that someone could store valuable stones, a few $100 bills, or a handful of gold coins in a safe, they might also keep their Bitcoin in a digital wallet on their computer.

Why Is Bitcoin Such a Volatile Currency?

The volatile nature of cryptocurrency can largely be attributed to the fact that the industry is still in its infancy. Because dealers are completely susceptible to sentiment, terror, and greed, you get these ludicrous market reactions. In addition, there are recently introduced standards and strategies that are continuously altering the market and producing extreme fluctuations in price. After that comes the media found on the internet.

It's this strange new thing where viral social patterns, like Money Road Wagers or Elon Musk for example, have a significant influence on cryptocurrency. This is a relatively new phenomenon. If Elon Musk includes the hashtag "Bitcoin" in his Twitter profile, there is a 10% probability that the price of Bitcoin will increase. Even if internet media has a unique potential to fascinate and enliven audiences, the influence that it has on the Bitcoin market is another reason why casual financial supporters should be cautious. In light of the trends on Twitter, I would ask that you refrain from investing any resources in cryptographic forms of money.

Bitcoin and other cryptographic forms of money should in any event be seen as more risky resources, according to Danial. This is because there is so little documented background information on these monetary systems, in contrast to more common forms of speculation. Because the possible reward comes with a larger risk, you should make sure that any interest in Bitcoin is remembered for the less secure and more powerful designation of your more broad portfolio.

Mining for Bitcoin

When it comes to Bitcoin, there is a finite supply of 21 million coins; nevertheless, Bitcoin sent out its first transaction in 2009, and not all of the coins have been distributed. Since Satoshi Nakamoto mined the "beginning square," the initial square of Bitcoin, there have been about 18 million more Bitcoin added to circulation out of a total of 21 million Bitcoin. Additionally, new gold is introduced into the market as a result of mining; but, when it comes to gold, it is difficult to determine exactly how much more needs to be discovered and mined.

An sophisticated mining procedure is used to locate new Bitcoin and make them available for trading. This process involves using a computation to get the exceptional hash of each new square, which is a very lengthy string of digits and characters. The only thing that constitutes a block is a collection of transactions that take place inside a certain time frame, and fresh squares are made available on an ongoing basis.

Each new square that is discovered via the mining mechanism unlocks a certain amount of bitcoin. This results in advantages for the people who uncover new squares, as well as fresh Bitcoin being made available to buyers. Excavators have programmed their own computers to make a large number of guesses per second in an effort to decipher the erratic codes, since there is no clear explanation for the hash value of each byte.

Excavators make use of powerful personal computers referred to as "hubs" in order to search for and locate additional squares.

Anyone may become a Bitcoin miner by using the free software that is available on Bitcoin.org; however, using a computer in this manner requires a significant amount of additional space and energy. The first person to decipher the code will be given the opportunity to create the next square, and they will also get the transaction fees associated with that Bitcoin when it is exchanged. A money box has been placed in each of the new squares. In addition to this, there is a square reward that consists of free Bitcoin that is released into the market.

The mining mechanism is just another component that contributes to Bitcoin's wildly unpredictable day-to-day volatility. According to Bloodsucker, there are around 900 Bitcoin added to the flow of circulation on a continuous basis via mining. However, Bitcoin's source code is made of a recurring pattern that is referred to be "dividing," and it can be found there. The amount of fresh Bitcoin that is always entering circulation is continuously split, much like a well-oiled clock.

The most recent Bitcoin chain split occurred in 2020, which means that the amount of Bitcoin entering circulation will be reduced once again in April or May of 2024. It is projected that the last Bitcoin will be produced in the year 2140, at which point the price will continue to fall until it reaches its all-time low.

Since Bitcoin was first introduced to the world, there have been several instances of this splitting, and each time, its acceptance has grown. Along these same principles, it is difficult to estimate the effects that splitting will have on the price of Bitcoin. The first division, which took place in 2012, was responsible for an increase in the value of Bitcoin, but the second division, which took place in 2016, was responsible for an initial decrease followed by an increase. The third Bitcoin fork, which took place in May 2020, did not have a significant impact on the price of Bitcoin, which has maintained record high prices ever since late 2020. A greater degree of price volatility is introduced into the market whenever Bitcoin is divided. It is designed to have a deflationary effect.

Deviation from the norm

Keep in mind the age-old question, "Is it a trend or will it bend?" Divergence is one method for determining this.

Now, up to this point, we have discussed trends, channels, as well as support and resistance. If you use them as a guide, you will be able to make some good successful transactions. However, there are moments when prices deviate from their tendencies.

That might take place for a wide variety of different causes. For example, this phenomenon may occur when a firm is added to a major market index, at which point large investment funds and exchange-traded funds are required to purchase the stock in order to maintain their positions in the index. Another possibility is that a company issues a profit warning that the market was not prepared for, causing the stock price to drop significantly below the range. There is also the possibility that a conflict would break out, or that some unforeseen political event will occur, either of which might send the market soaring or plunging. You may also see a major investor liquidating their holdings; for instance, in the case of initial public offerings (IPOs), the expiration of a lock-up period may result in the sale of some of the company's sponsors, founders, or management. It is also possible that it will occur "for no reason."

In point of fact, the reason for this is that each and every time the trendline has been challenged in the past, there have been buyers or sellers at the appropriate price to push the stock back up. This time, there were none of those things. And if that is the case, then it very certainly signals a modest shift in market mood, and there are a couple ways that you may pick up on that before the breakout. This is when points of divergence begin to emerge.

When you are analyzing the price chart for your asset, it is helpful to have a momentum indicator or a trade volume indicator (similar to an oscillator) running below it. (For the time being, you shouldn't think about what they signify; instead, focus on looking at the photos; we'll go over what they are and how they operate in more detail later.)

You'll see that the two lines go in very much the same direction most of the time. This is quite typical. If, on the other hand, the oscillator is moving in a downward direction when an uptrend is present, this is known as a negative divergence, and it indicates that the upswing may not continue.

On the other side, if the price recently set a new low but the momentum indicator is heading up, this indicates that prices could climb in the future; this is known as positive divergence.